The Lost and the Found

poems by

Mary Ellen Geer

Finishing Line Press
Georgetown, Kentucky

The Lost and the Found

ACKNOWLEDGMENTS

"Departure" was inspired in part by "The Brother and Sister" from Grimms' Fairy
Tales.
The Bashō haiku in "Moon-Viewing Room" was translated by Sam Hamill.
The two italicized lines in "December" are quoted from "Overheard on a
Saltmarsh" by Harold Monro.

Grateful thanks to my poetry community—the Henry Street poets, and the
invaluable ongoing poetry workshop of Suzanne Berger & company.

Publisher: Leah Maines

Editor: Christen Kincaid

Cover Art: "Blue Cup on Books" by Judith Prager,
www.pragerart.com

Author Photo: Philip LaFollette

Cover Design: Emily Arkin

Printed in the USA on acid-free paper.
Order online: www.finishinglinepress.com
                   also available on amazon.com

Author inquiries and mail orders:
Finishing Line Press
P. O. Box 1626
Georgetown, Kentucky 40324
U. S. A.

Table of Contents

The true paradises are the paradises that we have lost.

—Marcel Proust

Morning Thoughts on Evaporation

How quickly it all dries up—
the trees slick as butter just a moment ago,
each branch a slippery playground
for chickadee- and finch-feet;

then a burst of sun,
water steams gently off the trees, the grasses,
goes into the air and turns into something
weightless, the droplets so fine
I can barely see them.

How much is lost this way?
The stories these morning rains tell
of their cloud-origins, their intimacy
with wild winds and circling birds of prey;

my dreams as well, sharp as ice one minute,
the next moment gone, turned to mist,
rising up so high
even the birds have lost their memories.

I don't regret the bad ones, the nightmares,
my heart pounding as I try to part
the heavy curtains of fear;

but oh the beautiful ones,
the lovely threads of fantasy, the glimpses
of a world where colors are more intense,
where I greet the impossible
with mounting joy—

the dreams where I can soar without fear,
looking down at my tiny house,
watching the morning mist rise off the trees.

The Lost Map of New Jersey

Each one of us should make a surveyor's map of his lost fields and meadows.
In this way we cover the universe with drawings we have lived.
  —Gaston Bachelard

Meadows stitched with red-winged blackbirds
perched on reeds at the edge of the pond,
costumed with a startling patch of orange
on their glossy black wings;
cardinals, never again so brilliant and red
as in that bright time of childhood;
bluejays, the hoarse music of their cries
scintillating the pines on a clear fall day—

that whole lost countryside, not yet
all paved over, acres of woods
where a child could find mysterious rocks,
hidden caves, the past—

where she could almost hear the soft footfalls
of the ones who lived there
first, who gave the places their names,
Wyoming, Watchung, Whippany, Parsippany,
she could see them gliding between the trees,
heads bent as they listened to the birds, the snakes,
the stones, they understood the languages
of the natural world—they knew the secret
that all the years would conspire to lose.

While She Is Sleeping

It is August, the night is hot. In her room
at the top of the house, the girl sleeps
on rough cotton sheets. The house
is on a dusty road at the edge of the town—
it might be in Spain, or again, it might be
in South Carolina. She is thirteen.

Thin grey cats glide down secret pathways
between the houses, their glowing eyes
reflect the hot moon. Their voices rise
in strange melodies that caress the ears
of the sleeping girl—night-songs that slink
along the edges of her dreams.

Swifts dart through the moon-bright air,
in search of flying insects. They swoop up high
and sail back down, wings stretched wide,
forked tails tracing patterns in the sky.
The sleeping girl feels herself flying; she sails
the sky's pathways, drifts down to her bed.

The short summer night wears on, the moon
begins to sink. The cats cease their prowling,
lie down in rough grass; they dream of flying birds.
The swifts come to rest in the cottonwood trees;
a few diamond-shaped leaves drift down,
fall on the eyes of the sleeping girl. She wakes up.

The Latch

The watchers fan out,
silent as ghosts, following paths
that wind through the trees
like soft frayed ribbons made of moss
and mud. They are seeking

treasure—the speckled eggs
birds have laid in their nests—
not to plunder but to capture
their images. The only sounds
are light footfalls,
the soft click of shutters.

I walk behind them, hoping
they'll guide my steps,
but all they can find
are the gray and brown birds—
phoebe, finch, black-capped chickadee—
with their eggs of light blue,
off-white, beige, brown.

I'm looking for a flash of yellow,
so bright I'll see spots before my eyes
and have to look away.
I saw its picture in a book, now lost,
that I read over and over
when I was six. A bright yellow bird
with eggs like lemons.

Long after the other watchers
have gone, I keep searching
the well-worn paths.
If I can find the yellow bird,
she will show me a new path
in the heart of the woods—the smell
of lemons in the air, the shingled house,
the latch that opens the door, the book
with the blue cover, the picture,
all the years as nothing.

Moon-Viewing Room

I've been waiting through many months
        of full moons
I've been straining to see the moon
        through small windows
I've been patient, but moon-madness
        has overtaken me.

I will build a moon-viewing room
        on the back of my house
It will face the woods
        and the distant river
I will use whatever rough boards
        I can scavenge or steal.

Each wall will have two openings
        to frame the moon like a picture
Each wall will have a low bench
        running its length
There will be a railing too
        just the right height for elbows.

I will finish the room in time
        for the Long Night Moon
I will watch it travel through the sky
        printing moon-images on my eyes
I will stay up all night, drunk
        with moon watching.

I can see a V of geese flying high
        over the trees
I can see the river, glinting silver
        with reflected light
I can see Bashō in his boat, composing
        a poem in his head:

Just a cloud or two—
to rest the weary eyes
of the moon-viewer

Underneath

we build houses over dank holes in the ground
filled with leaf mold   roots and old bones

we rejoice as the walls go up   the floors   the roof
we decorate the walls with art   the floors with rugs

we don't see what's under the surface   all it takes
is a few forgetful days and mold will bloom

mice will gnaw a hole   they will sneak through
from below to eat our bread   they are waiting

for us to turn our heads   to look out the window
distracted by a flash of blue   we are careless

we squander the days   we decorate our bodies
with beautiful fabrics   silks and scarves

we imagine we are beautiful   we don't think
about what's under the skin   the cells slowly dying

we are careless   living on the surface
we look out the window   waiting for the flash of blue

What We Know By Now

That the way ahead is far from clear

That the path is narrow; on either side
only brackish water, mud, exploded flowers

That the broken birds can't tell us
which way to turn when the path forks

That we need a stronger light to pierce the fog

That night lasts longer than day

That the false promises of summer
left us dazed; we forgot the cold would come

That the children are still lost;
the signals from their video games
are faint and buzzing

That it is hard to hear each other

That even though the music
is getting louder, we have forgotten
how to sing

Sunflower

Dazzlement is all you show me
at first, extravagant wheel of yellow,

outsized, as if you've absorbed
the flowerness of all the others

into one huge disk, petals
whirling and circling, pointing

toward that other gold disk
in the sky. But when I look closely

there's more to you than yellow—
there's your dark heart, which I see

is really two hearts:
the brown seed-head, a darker circle

within the gold, whose edges bleed
into the yellow and cast a shadow

on the petals' inner ends,
turning them a brownish orange—

like the color that overspreads the sun
as it's going into eclipse—

then the innermost circle,
your dark eye, almost black, and what

do I see in it? Nothing, it is the void,
the darkness that has pulled

everything into itself, the place
where no colors can penetrate,

the place where I find myself,
shivering, when the sun has gone out.

Peonies

you want to escape
from the house, the small rooms,
the telephone calls
from your neighbor
who has nothing better to do
than voice her shrill complaints

your hands ache
from arthritis but you go
out to the yard, sink to your knees
in the yielding spring dirt,
rejoice in the peonies' tight buds,
the tiny red flame that will burn
at the heart of the white flower

you see the fur-flame of fox
streak across the yard,
her kits safe in their hole
near the back of the garage

every day the peonies open
a little more; the little foxes
venture farther from the den

one night the neighbor calls:
got them at last—
every year those foxes—
our cats weren't safe—
came with his shotgun—

you can't bear to go out,
the only dirt you can touch
is in flowerpots, tame
white blossoms of the begonias

in the yard
the peonies grow blowsy,
they lean their heavy heads over,
fall from their stems

blood on the grass

when you look out the window
you can no longer see
the white ghosts of the peonies,
their red hearts

In Balance

Stretched out on the sofa with a book
I know I'll love, every page still unread,
I look out the window at the golden light,
autumn trees half-undressed but still bright,
I know the cold is coming but not yet, not yet,
a breeze sifts through the open window,
lifts my hair, ruffles the pages of the book,
no hiss of steam heat yet, the air is light, sounds
of outdoors can still be heard, the mockingbird,
rustle of chipmunks in the leaves, the squirrels
hiding the acorns, soon enough they'll be digging
frantically in the cold, trying to find
where they buried them, but not yet, not yet,
all is still abundance, I start to read
and the gift of a free afternoon stretches
ahead of me, the hours unrolling and falling
gently downhill, the turning pages of the book,
I enter another life, the woman, her lover,
I think their story won't end well, their love
will never last, they'll have to part, but not yet,
not yet, right now it's all in balance,
the plot hasn't reached its tipping point,
I read on, the double images inhabit me,
the book, the light, the lovers, the leaves, the ease
of time stretched out, love not lost, no, not yet.

The Coming Winter

Light drains out of the sky
earlier now—the start
of the long shutting in.

Geese wait for the secret signal,
take off in a huge uproar,
flapping and honking.

The wind's new sharpness,
cold fingers lifting the edges
of a scarf.

*   *   *   *   *

Hardness of the ground,
no longer springy underfoot;
the brittle grass.

Bones of the landscape
now visible, hedges stripped
of their leaves.

The owl's sharp gaze
lays bare the hiding places
of the small rabbits.

*   *   *   *   *

The sounds, the music of summer—
birds, crickets, children's songs—
where are they?

Where are the children?
Changed by the cold, as in a fairy tale.
They are lost.

If they manage to find their way home,
what will they see?
Cold house, everyone sleeping.

The spell has been cast.

Departure

Sun glinting on the ice. Numbing wind.
Thin ribbon of river, channel of moving water
between borders of ice. The boat,
much too fragile for the journey ahead.
The frozen day, not auspicious.

The brother and sister, getting ready
to leave. Wrapped in warm cloaks
the mother has pressed on them.
Their honey-colored hair gleaming
in the sun, ruffled by the wind.
Their amusement at their mother's fussing,
the casual way they tell her
everything will be fine.

The instructions, the spells:
how to make nourishing soup
from a few simple ingredients;
how to fold laundry; how to tell
one's true love from a deceiver;
how to foil the dark arts
and the snares of wicked witches;
how to know whether the water in a stream
is pure, or is poisoned by an evil spell.
Now the last words to her daughter:

If the worst happens, if your brother
drinks from a poisoned stream
and is turned into a deer,
never leave him;
untie your ribbon of woven gold
and put it around his neck;
lead him through the woods
to a small cottage; stay with him
through many seasons, summers
and snowfalls, until the spell is broken
and he resumes his human form.

Sun glinting on the ice. Loud rush of wings,
a wild duck taking off, the mother distracted
by the sudden movement. When she looks again
the boat is already moving, they are waving
and smiling. The river carries them downstream;
she gazes after them with longing
till the boat dwindles to a small speck.

The Bride, the Hawk, and the Moon

October sun comes out
after morning's rain,
floods the river-meadow,
turns it bronze-gold;
late afternoon light
pours over the grasses
like honey from a jar;
leaves quiver in the wind
and glow like candles.

A bride appears
with her husband,
posing for pictures
on the wooden bridge,
silk dress trailing
on rough boards.
The moon hangs low
in the still-light sky,
and a twin moon,
the photographer's silver disk
behind the couple,
makes the good luck double,
like a Chinese fortune.

At dusk a hawk
touches down at the top
of a copper beech,
waiting, watchful.
A mouse moves in the grass,
and he dives—
the way winter comes
and kills off fall;
the way a careless betrayal
puts an end to love.

Amber

You thought I was beautiful,
so you came too close to me.
How could you resist my glow,
how you could turn away when I was still
so soft, so molten?

Did you think a common lacewing
would be beneath my notice?
I was mesmerized by the glistening green
of your gorgeous wings.

For a while it was wonderful—
when you could still move,
when I could feel your wings
fluttering in my soft depths.
Why did I give in
to my desire to imprison you?
I couldn't help holding you
tighter and tighter.

And then one day you were still.

What power I had, to harden
around you, to keep you
young forever, your body unchanged—
your long thin antennae, the perfection
of your round black eye.

But never again will I see your lace-bright wings
flying toward me, glittering in the morning sun;

never again will you feel the small night rain
falling on the folded flower of your wings.

Tree Swallows

The way they dart and skim, the patterns
their forked tails trace on the sky;
the way their dark backs flash iridescent blue
in the sun; the way they conceal
their white underbellies, like a secret;
the way they can swoop down
from high in the sky and find
the portal that takes them
from outside to home—all this I know
intimately, the way I know my own body,
its warm places and its cool places,
its secrets. Now I am flying with them,
I can speak their language, I think
this will last forever—but my other life
calls, and as soon as I leave them
and go inside, I understand nothing.

In Search of Lost Nights

all I wanted was the moon
silvery beams lighting my room
driving out the dark   I wanted
to sail through the window
and fly with her, gliding past
Orion and Gemini, staying up
all night, finally sinking into the trees
resting there, watching the sun rise

now nights are for sleeping
or lying awake, restless
fears buzzing around my head
like a cloud of insects   wanting
to remember, to forget

where are those wild nights
that feeling of opening up
expanding into the sky
flying with the moon, fearless
becoming silver

Lullaby

Lie down on your soft bed,
the sheets so smooth,
the quilt so comforting.
Listen to the breeze
stirring the leaves of the aspen.
Watch the golden roundness
of the moon through the skylight.
Think of the soft woolly sheep,
sheltered in the meadow's fold.

Lie down on your warm bed,
cradled by flannel sheets,
the quilt hovering just above.
Listen to October's wind,
leaves drifting down from the aspen.
Watch the orange harvest moon
as it climbs through the sky.
Think of the good gray sheep,
patient in the cool meadow.

Lie down on your hard bed,
the sheets beginning to fray,
quilt parting at the seams.
Listen to the wind rip
the quivering leaves off the aspen.
Watch the moon, its light
casting weird shadows on the wall.
Think of the tangled sheep,
huddled together against the cold.

Lie down on your ravaged bed,
sheets worn to thin ribbons,
quilt in tatters. Listen to the wind
as it batters the side of the house;
see the aspen, naked and cold.
Watch the moon, flying
too low—cover your head.
Think of the sheep, half frozen—
by morning, some of them dead.

December

her glittering, luminous body
the light   crescent
moon-night   the black velvet
sky the pinpricks   the vast cold

cold shrinking of the year
the dwindling   only a few
sparks left   not a waxing but
a waning her life so small now
the candle almost out
what did she forget
to tell me   the end of the story

stories we tell ourselves
about our lives   how we weave them
out of thinnest tissue   so many
lies   so much invention   she knows
all the parts I left out

out of her body I came
rush of water   what did I know
about life's mysteries
the water the comets brought
oceans   my story just beginning
what did I know

what I knew in the beginning
words she gave me
more words   stories   poems
they are better than stars or water
hush, I stole them out of the moon

moon   light in the darkness
cold night   the candle guttering
almost out now
end of the story never told
the dwindling, the dimming
her thin, luminous body

Copper Beech

How many knives have pierced your limbs,
the small sharp cuts of those who wanted
their names joined forever in a heart?

How many children have found
a secret hiding place
under your wide, sheltering branches?

How many winters have you stood,
solid and patient as an elephant, enduring
the winds, the sleet, even the loss
of your beautiful coppery crown?

Today the air is full of loss,
fall beginning its slide toward winter;
I seek you out in your meadow
at the edge of the slow-moving river.

Hold me like a mother, now that mine
is losing her frail grip; look at me,
bear witness to my smallest acts,
listen to all the stories
I've made up about my life.

Take my poems, the ones she loved to read;
hang them from your branches,
let them flutter like little flags in the wind,
let them be your leaves through the long winter.

Holding

The clay pot holds the flower,
the mouth of the flower holds
the hummingbird's beak.

The world is profligate
with holding. The sky
holds the moon, the house
embraces the family,
the child grasps the spoon.

You and I hold hands
as we walk through the woods,
children long gone.
Gray moss hangs from the trees
like beards. The nurse log
cradles the young seedlings.

We are in a holding pattern.
Who knows
how much time is left to us
in this life.

Hold me close against you
on this cold night,
enfold me as tightly
as the eggcup holds the egg.
Let us pretend
nothing will ever change.
The world is flush
with holding, it can spare
some for us.

The Words She Spoke

One morning, three weeks after his death,
she opened her mouth and a bird flew out.

It was small, a black-capped chickadee
that sang *hey sweetie, hey sweetie,*

and the people around her didn't
really notice, kept drinking their coffee

as the bird hopped from table to table,
calling for its mate.

All day she kept quiet, not wanting
to attract attention, but the next day

when she ordered her coffee
and tried a soft "good morning,"

another bird flew out, startling the couple
sitting near her. She wanted

to keep her loss to herself, it was *hers,*
but after days of not speaking

she could no longer bear the silence.
As she walked through the city

she began to notice there were others:
a boy who had lost his mother

and could only produce plump robins;
a man who uttered a cloud of golden finches.

She started to seek them out,
wanting to share whatever it was

that was happening to them. Some nights
they would meet in an old warehouse,

standing together in the dim light,
watching the birds circle high under the roof,

all of them strangely comforted
by the new language they were learning.

The House Where Lost Things Are Found

I open the door. A fine layer of dust
over the tables, the chairs.
On a schoolgirl's desk, a book
that's been missing since I was ten—
its cover warped, colors faded, the story
still vivid in my mind: the evil troll-king
who guards the tunnels under the mountain;
the brave girl, lost in the maze,
who finds the thread that will lead her out.

I follow the thread through many rooms.
In the first, on a scuffed wooden dresser,
a thin gold ring rimmed with tiny stones,
the one my grandmother gave me
that I lost, spent hours searching for
in the cracks between the floorboards.
In another room, my favorite purple scarf.
I find my cracked blue cup, my diary,
my canary that left its cage and flew away.

In the last room a girl sits reading
by a sunny window, rocking in a tall chair,
turning the pages of the troll-king book,
stopping every now and then to admire
the way her gold ring glitters in the light.

I long to stay in the warmth of that room,
to read until the shadows lengthen
and my book comes to its end,
all danger overcome. But I know
I have to leave. I close the door,
feel for the thread in the dim hallway,
and begin the slow journey
that will lead me back to the present—

to the only life I have,
with its lost rings, its disappearing birds,
its plots that don't end well,
its beautiful confusions.

Mary Ellen Geer is a Boston-area poet and editor. Before her recent retirement, she worked for 26 years at Harvard University Press as a manuscript editor and production editor. She edited both scholarly and general-interest books in a wide variety of fields, including literary criticism, musicology, history, and popular culture.

Mary Ellen grew up in New Jersey and in Bennington, Vermont, and is a graduate of Wellesley College. A lifelong reader of poetry and novels, she first developed a serious interest in writing poetry through taking workshops at the Harvard Extension School and the Fine Arts Work Center in Provincetown. Her poetry has been deepened and enriched by her participation since 2009 in Suzanne Berger's excellent poetry workshop, as well as by her writing group, the Henry Street Poets.

Mary Ellen's poems have appeared in several publications including *The Comstock Review, Slant,* and *The Charles River Review.* She is the author of two previous chapbooks, *At the Edge of the Known World* and *Life/Afterlife,* both published by Finishing Line Press. In 2008 her poem "How to Write a Sestina" was the winner of the New England Poetry Club's Boyle/Farber Award for a poem in a traditional form.

When she is not writing poetry or reading, Mary Ellen enjoys hiking and choral singing. She lives in Acton, Massachusetts, with her husband Philip.

www.ingramcontent.com/pod-product-compliance
Lightning Source LLC
LaVergne TN
LVHW041329080426
835513LV00008B/645